ENTREPRENEURS & INVESTORS

INNOVATIVE, SCALABLE AND VIABLE BUSINESS SUGGESTIONS

Contents

Set Up Your Business In The UK
Innovative, scalable and viable business suggestions

Setting up and doing business in the United Kingdom is projected to be business as usual. Brexit or no Brexit, deal or no deal, Britain will continue to maintain its immaculate position as a global business hub. With no Brexit, the United Kingdom will play its role per usual. In the event of Brexit, it will open up more avenues and opportunities for dealing with countries directly.

'Made in Britain' and 'the British' will continue to extend assurance in terms of quality and class. Though certain geo-political and socio-economic realignments and combining of new partnerships will materialise, in either case of Brexit or no-Brexit, the UK will remain a pivotal business partner for the EU and other countries alike.

The very location of the UK will remain strategic if viewed as a stepping stone to approaching the huge market of over 1.3 billion people. The UK will remain an active market of over 60 million people, coupled with the EU population of over 500 million, making well over 560 million in total. To the West, the UK is the gateway to the USA, Canada, Brazil, Argentina, Mexico, Chile and other Latin American countries, with an estimated population of over 790 million.

Rising local population coupled with global challenges such as environment, climate change, health, economy, human rights, good governance and social justice, offers a huge opportunity to conceive and create new and innovative solutions, and introduce improvements to existing services. Each solution and service is in fact an innovative, viable and scalable business in its own right, with the UK providing the perfect hotbed for launching businesses both by local residents and those settling from abroad.

With so many opportunities on offer, identifying available business options and choosing the right one that is specific to the individual is the key to opening a new world of business and opportunities for the investor, the entrepreneur and shareholders.

This guide aims to provide a starting point that will lead to the launch of commercially successful businesses in the UK.

Easy to read, this Book highlights Business Opportunities and Business Ideas appropriate for the UK, supported by examples of existing businesses to help readers gather information on the business that we have chosen and to help understand products, services, business models, pricing, marketing and other essentials. Ideal Book for Entrepreneurs and those who wish to launch their business in the United Kingdom.

United Kingdom is an Ideal Place to Launch a Business

Local UK- to regional European Union-wide and internationally, the United Kingdom has achieved significance through decades and centuries. In the business sphere, the UK is a significant focal point for investors and entrepreneurs nationally and internationally. From research & development and funding to protection of intellectual rights, the UK covers it all. Key attributes of what makes the UK an ideal place to launch a Business include[ii]::

Clusters
Many Enterprise Zones have employment clusters, where businesses from the same sector are co-located within the zones.

FDI
For Inward Investment in Europe, UK is No 1.

Funding
Opportunities exist for Government grants, finance and loans, and Start-up or Small- and Medium-sized Enterprise funding.

Governmental Support
Department for International Trade can help overseas companies looking to locate or invest in the UK by offering free services.

Ideal Location
New or existing customers, closer proximity to product innovation and development, and support for finding new suppliers and partners.

Infrastructure Development
Transport improvements: A £120 billion investment programme is helping to improve our transport systems. The UK already has the second-largest ports industry in Europe, largest air transport system in Europe, and most improved rail network in the EU.

Intellectual Property
Strong supply chain and strong distribution infrastructure.

Locations
Different locations across the UK known as Enterprise Zones offer investors incentives to locate; reduced taxes, simpler planning rules and financial benefits.

Patented Inventions
Companies can apply a lower rate of Corporation Tax on profits from patented inventions and certain innovations.

Research & Development
R&D tax credits: Companies may get a 100% deduction of Corporation Tax on work related to R&D.

Skills & Workforce
The UK has a workforce of over 30 million people, the second-largest in the EU.

Tax
Corporation Tax 20%; joint-lowest in the G20, the world's largest 20 economies.

Choosing a Business
Essential considerations

Starting up a business starts with choosing a Business Idea. The first question to answer is 'Which Business Should I Start?'.

To answer this, we should consider a few core issues:

We start by focusing on our *passion*, what moves us, what drives us to succeed in life, and what we most enjoy doing, day after day. We may have an interest in electricals, electronics or gaming and designing, drawing or performing arts; whatever our passion , we must start by searching the business closest to it. A business that most closely aligns with our passion is the business we should go for. No business sails without any hiccups, headwinds and ups and downs during its lifecycle.

We may possess a *skill* developed through our education qualifications, working experience, observation, cultural and social background, or our upbringing. A business that utilizes our skill should be our choice.

In launching a business in a territory new to us, our initial research should be into finding out the *preferences of local government*. Almost everywhere, local governments promote certain industries or espouse policies which impact positively on some businesses and negatively on others. Examining local government strategies is an appropriate starting point here.

In selecting a *city* to set up our business we need to research those businesses or industries linked to that city. Almost every city gives some prominence to certain businesses; for instance, tourism will flourish more readily in seaside areas such as Blackpool, Liverpool, Brighton and Southend-On-Sea. By comparison, the best choice in Edinburgh is an enterprise based on arts and culture. Even within the major metropolises of London, Birmingham and Manchester, the actual locality within a city showcases specific business ideas that succeed for specific areas: food outlets, cinemas, travel and tours are quite common. But if we zoom in more closely, we see that West London may be a good location for botanical and horticultural business, while East London is more inclined towards fashion; South London is a music paradise and North London may well be a digital heaven.

In considering a successful business start-up for us, we need to understand that every business comes with its own specific *success model* and structure, such as Uber Eats backed by the giant Uber. This is based on a highly evolved big enterprise model and should not be considered as an 'easy' option. Before being tempted into a specific successful business we need to review the backing businesses and the investors who in most cases are in fact the real reasons for the business. Therefore success in a business can be attributed not only to the business itself, but also many other factors.

Designing an *Exit strategy* is always a part of structured business planning. No business comes with complete certainty and assurance as to its success. A strategy to exit when our business does not turn out to be as successful as originally planned paves the way to save the business from sustaining any losses.

And just which kind of business will cost less in overall terms if exiting is the best choice? Obviously, any business with *low operating costs*. This is why we have to carefully consider exactly how much money to invest into operations in the first place, and also as the business develops and grows along the way. That money is not going to come back. By contrast, any investment made in property or tangible assets may have potential for recovery.

Many authorities offer *tax benefits* to certain businesses, industries and initiatives, such as those involving research, which attracts tax reliefs from tax authorities. Tax relief has a direct impact on distributable profits. High-tax relief businesses attract investors and the investment.

Innovative and creative businesses are less competitive by default, therefore penetration into the market attracts limited or relatively no resistance.

With the advent of the Internet and ecommerce platforms, setting up a local business with global outreach has become relatively easier. The first step is to align your business idea with whatever is important globally, such as the needs of global communities, benefit of regional, national and international people of one or more countries. Align your business with subjects of global importance such as environment, greenhouse gases, CO2, climate change, crime, social media, economy and economic challenges, social issues, famine, flooding, extinction of species, global education, literacy, drinking water, malaria, type II Diabetes, cholesterol, heart attack, emotional health, creating talent, cyber-security, smart cities, lifting

out of poverty, fintech, biosciences, and conflicts.

Add *technological solutions* to your idea to give it mass appeal and mass penetration in global markets.
Find existing services and create ways to improve on them **efficiently and with ease**.

Business could *target a specific age group, gender, ethnicity or political wisdom*. In such a situation, outreach to more of countries would be required.

Business should have a *scale of impact* as well as a scale of expansion.

A business should be seen to constantly grow and expand. Starting with the *viability* of the business, the business idea must be able to turn out to be commercially viable and sustainably growing. For growth, one vital aspect is *scalability*. From just a small business in a small neighbourhood, the business should view scalability as the next target. Beyond scalability, *innovation* will take the business to higher levels in its future.

Best businesses are those which cannot be *replicated* by potential competitors, or businesses which competition will find it difficult to enter and compete in.

Success or failure of an existing operation does not assure a similar fate for any other competitor. This is because each business collates its own set of dynamically variable factors such as owner, related visions, commitment, staff suitability, location dynamics, market and customers. Therefore, a successful business replica can still turn out to be a failure. Tools to success vary from business to business, however they can include the business name, the colour scheme you choose, the front office staff, the first impressions customers get, etc. The UK is unsurprisingly a new market for those coming from abroad and equally may well be new for those who are local; in either case, launching a brand-new business in an already crowded market is a challenge.

It is a given that all business launches involve considerable input of *time,* but more importantly a major investment of *skill and money.*

Most of all, we want a business we can be *proud* to be associated with, a business which *encourages* us to drive it forward and work hard on to make it a success and grow.

Location is a prime choice for any start-up: either identify a location then select a business suitable for that location or identify a business and find a suitable location for it. Works well either way.

A location where we can source suitable *staff* easily is more ideal than a location where staff cannot be found conveniently. Or if we can make it easy for staff to relocate to our location, then it would be still be good for the business.

Pre-Launch Essentials

Feasibility Report, Business Plan and Financial Projections are the major three documents which define, design and drive the business to be launched. *Feasibility Report* assesses the viability of the business idea, the break-even point, the sensitivity analysis, and customers' choices, preferences, trends; the *Business Plan* provides a roadmap for the business to operate on; and the *Financial Projections* show the costs and payments, income and receipts, cash and profits in the foreseeable future. All three documents are based on extensive *Market Research* including competition and competitor analysis.

Investment Opportunities in British Industries

Industries from Manufacturing to Aerospace, Agri-tech and Asset Management to Energy and Food offer enormous opportunities for investors to invest, and for entrepreneurs to launch businesses.

Industry highlights[iii]:

Advanced Manufacturing

- £168 billion contributed to UK economy 74.5 million GBP of investment in high-value manufacturing projects
- 80 billion Euro worth of funding for research and development between 2014 and 2020
- set to grow in 3D printing, composites, sensors and data analytics.

Aerospace

- £31 billion annual turnover 17% of the entire global aerospace market supplied by UK manufacturing
- £1.95 billion investment in research and development available in 2013 - 2026
- National Aerospace Technology Exploitation Programme - a £40 million programme supporting 250 SMEs to develop new R&D.

Agri-tech

- Plant science
- Animal health
- Precision agriculture
- Aquaculture
- The UK is a global centre of excellence for agri-tech R&D and innovation
- Overseas companies have:
- support from government to improve competitiveness in the agri-

tech sector, as part of the £160 million UK Strategy for Agricultural Technologies
- access to world-leading researchers
- access to a fully integrated agricultural food supply chain worth £96 billion annually
- government financial support.

Asset Management

- 7 years of successive growth
- UK is one of the world's most accessible markets for asset management
- total funds under management across the industry increased to a record £8.1 trillion in 2016
- high potential growth.

Automotive

- First in Europe for ease of doing business, 100 international markets buy from the UK automotive industry - totalling £40 billion in exports in 2016
- UK specialises in motorsports and car manufacturing
- world-class research and development Catapult centre.

Communications

- The UK communications sector has about 8000 companies employing over 270,000 people

- The UK's mobile market is the largest in Europe with a value of £14 billion annually and 80 million mobile subscribers.
- By 2015 the value of transactions made through mobile devices was estimated at €81.9 billion.

Creative
- Two million workers employed in UK creative industries largest design industry in Europe
- £1.6 billion spent on film production in 2016
- 25% tax breaks for foreign film companies moving to the UK.

Electronics and IT Hardware

Electronics
- The electronics sector is worth £16 billion every year to the UK economy
- about 300,000 people in over 12,000 companies.

Consumer Electronics
- The UK is the largest European market for high-end consumer electronics products
- about 18,000 UK-based companies.

Power Electronics
The UK's strength and future opportunities for power electronics are in 4 main areas:
- transport
- energy generation
- transmission and distribution
- consumer electronics

Semiconductors and Electronic Design
The UK has a 40% share of Europe's electronics design industry.

Design
The UK has 150 independent electronic system design houses, more than any other European country.

Medical Electronics
- There are over 3000 companies in the UK medical devices sector
- a turnover of over £13 billion.

Communications
- The UK has the largest personal communications market in Europe
- Communications made up 20% of the total European semiconductor industry in 2010.

Automotive Electronics
- The automotive market accounted for 22% of the total European semiconductor industry in 2010
- The UK is one of 5 major automotive manufacturing countries in Europe
- Produces over 1 million vehicles
- manufactures more than 2 million engines annually.

Defence Electronics
- UK government and military purchases accounted for 1% of the total European semiconductor market in 2010.
- The UK is the second-largest defence exporter.

Security Electronics
- The UK is the world's largest market for intelligent transport systems (ITS) and surveillance-related technologies.
- It has over 25% of the world's CCTV installations in the UK.

Energy-Efficient Lighting and Displays
- The UK commercial and domestic lighting market is worth around £1 billion
- more than 1700 companies work in the lighting supply chain
- More than 500 semiconductor businesses are in the UK
- 80% of these are foreign-owned companies
- employ more than 8000 engineering staff.

Energy Generation
- £200 billion total cost of energy projects; UK's location offers advantages for wind, wave, oil and gas opportunities
- growth in low-carbon industries
- access to world-class engineering workforce.

Financial Technology
- 76,500 people employed in UK fintech sector - one of the world's largest
- In 2015, the fintech sector turnover was about £6.6 billion
- attracted about £524 million in investment
- 40,000 people are employed UK-wide
- the sector attracts more fintech investment and talent than anywhere else in Europe.

Food and Drink Manufacturing
- £110 billion contributed in 2015
- UK consumer spend £230bn
- strong demands for new products
- 8500 new products are added to supermarkets each year
- Europe's 743 million consumers are within easy reach of the UK

- Information Communications Technology
- The UK develops software for many applications and international companies provide funding for research and development (R&D)
- About 100,000 software companies operate in the UK, including Microsoft, IBM and HP.

Mobile Device Market
- largest in Europe
- a value of £14 billion annually
- 80 million mobile subscriptions.

Cloud Computing
- The UK cloud-computing market is predicted to reach £6.1 billion by 2014 (source: TechMarketView)
- offers big investment opportunities for companies in the ICT sector
- 18% of UK small-medium enterprises (SMEs) use cloud
- 30% plan to use it in the next 12 months
- 81% of established cloud users in the UK plan to increase cloud usage over the next 2 years.

Data Centres
Many companies in the UK are looking to outsource their data centres, recognising the need to locate their data nearer to their customers and employees worldwide.

Cyber Security
- Secure networks are important for the security of the UK and other countries
- The UK is a leader in providing secure communications and offers companies opportunities in areas including cyber security

- The UK's cyber security market is worth about £2.8 billion.

Life Sciences
- Over 1000 life sciences companies driving £10 billion into Northern Powerhouse
- life sciences in the North of England contribute £10.8 billion to the UK economy each year
- over 1000 life sciences businesses in the North support over 38,000 high-skilled jobs
- Northern Powerhouse companies export over £8.1 billion of medicinal and pharma products per year.

Marine Energy
- Wave and tidal energies
- The UK's coastline is more than 19,000 miles (30,500km) long.
- The UK is responsible for 27% of tidal energy developments and 23% of wave projects worldwide.

Energy Parks
The government encourages joining and grouping activities through marine energy parks.

Offshore Wind
- 10GW generated by UK offshore wind by 2020; already 5.7 gigawatts (GW) of offshore wind installed or under construction.
- on track to deliver 10GW by 2020 - this represents the largest expansion in any class of renewable energy technology in the UK
- home to the world's largest operational offshore wind farm, London Array (630 megawatts).

Oil and Gas
- 22 billion barrels of recoverable oil reserves remain
- Over 380 fields are producing oil and gas in the UK today
- 43 billion barrels of oil being recovered from the UK Continental Shelf
- With over 100 years' experience, businesses can be sure they're entering a market widely acknowledged as a global leader
- There are over 350,000 people in the industry, including 50,000 experts in subsea production.

Rail Industry
- Today, nearly 20% of all European passenger journeys take place within the UK
- As a significant driver in the UK economy, the rail industry accounts for expenditure of around £12 billion per year
- A world-class Rail Network
- Track 32,000 km
- Stations 2500; Trains 4000
- Daily Services 20,000
- Passenger travel 58 billion km
- Passenger Journeys 1.5 billion
- Freight 110 billion tonnes.

Retail
- Third in the world for online business-to-consumer sales
- third in the world for online consumer sales - the largest e-commerce market in Europe
- a luxury goods market estimated to reach £96 billion by 2018
- world-renowned heritage and high-quality brands.

Space Technology
- The UK's space industry contributes £9.1 billion to the economy
- employs over 29,000 highly skilled people.
- over 260 companies in the industry
- the last few years have seen average annual company growth of 10%.

Satellite Communications
The UK has a 20% share of the global telecoms satellite market.

Earth Observation
The UK is a partner in all the major Earth observation programmes in Europe including being the largest supplier of Earth observation satellite training programmes.

Space Security
UK companies provide the UK's defence department with secure communications, allowing military operations on land, sea and air to be controlled anywhere.

Successes in UK Space Work
- The last 4 years have seen big success in the industry
- UK government help for industry
- In 2013 the UK government announced a £200 million investment to develop the latest space technology
- This included £60 million investment in SABRE - a British-designed rocket engine which could revolutionise air travel and reduce the cost of reaching space.
- £134 million contract for space technology company Astrium to develop instruments for the next generation of weather satellites - this is a direct result of the UK's increased investment in the European Space Agency.

Waste Management
- The UK's waste management industry has an annual turnover of £9 billion
- 70,000 people employed in the sector in 3000 companies
- The way waste is treated is important for material security, energy, climate change and environmental protection
- The UK deals with waste a number of ways, including:
- 40% of household waste recycled; 52% of commercial and industrial waste recycled or reused; 55% of local waste sent to landfill sites.

Low-Carbon Economy
The UK is focused on designing and developing a low-carbon solution.

EU Landfill Directive
It's estimated that the UK requires £8 billion in investment to meet 2020 landfill diversion targets.

Opportunities
- Infrastructure opportunities
- Packaging opportunities
- Waste type opportunities.

Business Scene in the United Kingdom

Business in the UK is as usual. Across England, Scotland, Wales and Northern Ireland businesses cover a wide range of trades and industries. Over the years, each industry registers growth, but sometimes declines in output and revenue.

An overview of the number of registered businesses, industries and growth is presented below, showing how industries and regions are performing from 2016 to 2018.

Number of Companies

As a matter of latest record, the number of companies and public corporations has continued to rise during 2017 – 18.
45.8% of corporate businesses are single-employee limited companies.

Business by Industry

Numbers of UK-registered businesses by broad industry group for 2016-18:

	Figures to the nearest thousand					
	2016	%	2017	%	2018	%
Agriculture, forestry and fishing	148	5.8	148	5.5	149	5.6
Production	146	5.7	149	5.6	150	5.6
Mining, quarrying and utilities	13	0.5	14	0.5	14	0.5
Manufacturing	133	5.2	135	5.1	136	5.1
Construction	302	11.8	320	12.0	332	12.4
Wholesale and retail; repair of motor vehicles	370	14.5	375	14.1	380	14.2
Motor trades	73	2.9	75	2.8	76	2.8
Wholesale	104	4.1	103	3.9	103	3.8
Retail	192	7.5	197	7.4	202	7.6
Transport and storage (incl. postal)	93	3.6	109	4.1	109	4.1
Accommodation and food services	148	5.8	150	5.6	153	5.7
Information and communication	207	8.1	217	8.1	219	8.2
Finance and insurance	52	2.1	56	2.1	58	2.2
Property	91	3.6	93	3.5	96	3.6
Professional, scientific and technical	459	18.0	479	17.9	468	17.5
Business administration and support services	208	8.2	228	8.6	224	8.4
Public administration and defence	7	0.3	7	0.3	7	0.3
Education	42	1.6	48	1.8	44	1.6
Health	113	4.4	120	4.5	108	4.1
Arts, entertainment, recreation and other services	168	6.6	169	6.3	171	6.4
TOTAL	2,555	100	2,669	100	2,669	100

Source: Office for National Statistics; Value Added Tax and/or Pay As You Earn

Growth by Industry

During 2017-18, industries were driven by a variety of increases and decreases. Health and Education decreased as against a huge growth for the previous year. The mining, quarrying and utilities, and finance and insurance industries showed substantial growth in 2018. The graph below shows the increase and decrease in different industries for 2017-18.

Figure 3: Percentage growth by industry

UK, 2017 to 2018

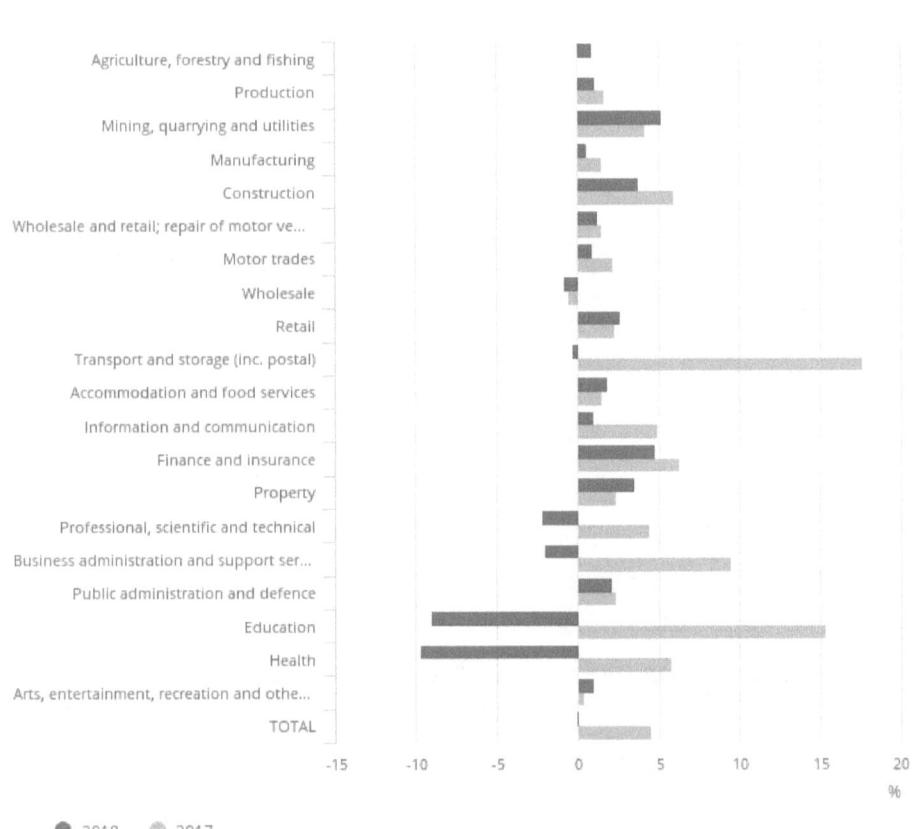

Source: **Office for National Statistics**

14

Business by Region

Numbers of registered businesses for 2016, 2017 and 2018 per region and percentage change:

	2016	%	2017	%	2018	%
					Figures to the nearest thousand	
North East	68	2.7	70	2.6	69	2.6
North West	245	9.6	260	9.7	268	10.0
Yorkshire and The Humber	178	7.0	185	6.9	183	6.9
East Midlands	173	6.8	177	6.6	179	6.7
West Midlands	201	7.9	213	8.0	213	8.0
East	254	9.9	271	10.2	264	9.9
London	477	18.7	506	18.9	506	19.0
South East	392	15.3	404	15.1	405	15.2
South West	227	8.9	234	8.8	232	8.7
Wales	100	3.9	103	3.8	104	3.9
Scotland	172	6.7	175	6.5	175	6.5
Northern Ireland	69	2.7	71	2.6	73	2.7
TOTAL	2,555	100	2,669	100	2,669	100
Source: Office for National Statistics						

Growth by Region

During 2017-18, Northern Ireland recorded the greatest percentage increase in number of registered businesses. The East England region had shown the highest percentage increase last year.

The graph below shows regions and increases and decreases in registered businesses.

Figure 4: Percentage growth by region

UK, 2017 to 2018

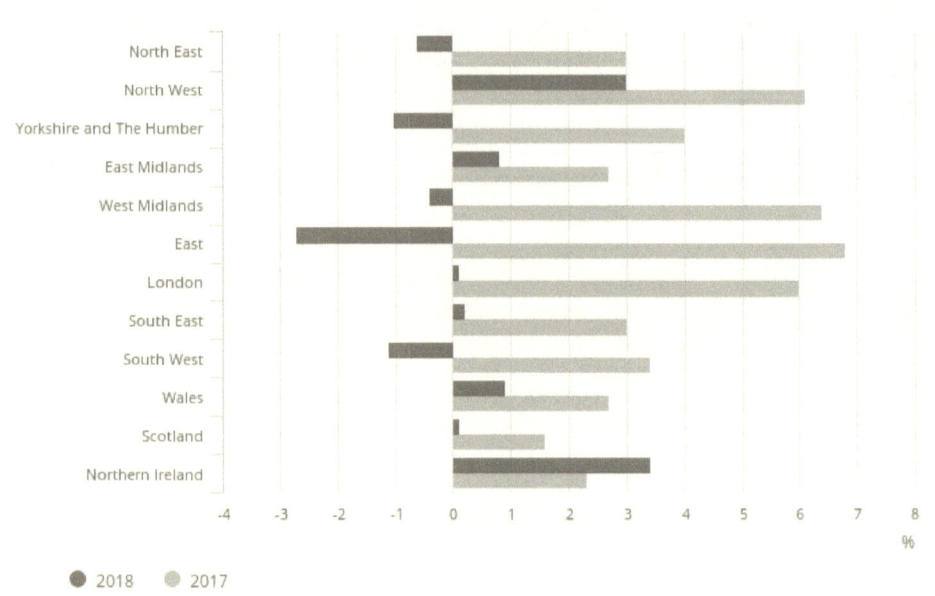

● 2018   ● 2017

Source: Office for National Statistics

16

Business Suggestions

As the UK is a land of opportunities, almost every sphere of business is represented here, from traditional and conventional to inventive, innovative and creative.

The following are examples of businesses currently operating in the UK:

A

Artificial Intelligence

Adbrain: Using machine learning algorithms to contextualize unstructured data points across devices, people, and households, Adbrain powers marketers and their tech partners to understand and engage with their customers across devices, channels and platforms.

Audio Books

Calibre Audio Books: Calibre Audio Library brings the pleasure of reading to people with sight problems, dyslexia or disabilities that prevent them from reading print. Calibre has almost 11,000 books to choose from, including 3000 especially for children and young people.

Automobiles

Fiat sees very significant opportunities for partnerships with other automakers mostly in the areas of autonomy and electrification projects. Fiat will spend $2 billion over the next three years on regulatory emissions credits. Tougher emissions regulations force the automaker to spend more on electrification.

Agricultural Robotics

Iron Ox - A maker of agricultural robots and John Deere are investing in artificial intelligence to raise produce more efficiently. The top use of the intelligence and the robotics is to cultivate time- and labour-intensive greens such as lettuce.

Aircraft Seating

Acro Aircraft Seating - Designing and manufacturing seats for airline passengers.

Advanced Materials

Tenmat - Manufacturer of advanced materials and components including wear parts and bearings, engineering ceramics, high-temperature-resistant materials, hard metals, and passive fire-protection solutions.

Alternative Energy

Soltropy - Captures sun's energy to support water-heating needs. Uniquely the system is ice-immune, has flexible modules and easily integrates with standard heating systems and components. Soltropy is a pioneer in simplified Solar Thermal technology for water-heating applications.

Aviation Systems
Inzpire - Experts in aviation and suppliers of defence-managed services, training, and the cutting-edge GECO Mission System and EFB.

Business turnaround service

B

Alvarez & Marsal solves operational, financial and regulatory challenges of leading companies, financial institutions and public entities and provides turnaround management solutions. A&M provides performance improvement and growth services. A&M also provides comprehensive restructuring and turnaround services, from simple advisory to interim and crisis management, fiduciary and insolvency services.

Business Cost-saving Service
Specialist Cost Auditors, a consulting practice helping businesses across the UK and Ireland reduce costs, save money and perform better. As a part of a cost-saving exercise, the firm examines payroll, operating costs, overheads and equipment costs and more. Its clients include Hilton Group, Mount Charles Catering, Queens Hotel, Portview Construction and many more.

Business Intelligence
Amplyfi - Business intelligence through machine-driven analysis. Technology horizon scanning, competitor intelligence, in-country risk assessments, strategy, continuous monitoring for disruptions, M&A Due Diligence, Venturing scouting, new entrant identification and strengthened credit assessment.

Bikes
Kinesis - Creates bikes, bike frames, wheels and components for road, adventure, cyclocross and mountain bikes that excel in UK riding conditions.

Business & Accounting Software
Xero - Business and accounting software.

Bike Tours
H & I Adventures – international mountain bike tours, guided mountain bike tours, combination of physical challenges and cultural adventures. The route, the tracks, the accommodation, the food, the flow of the day, the flow of the week. Epic scenery, wonderful food, great company.

Cosmetics

C

Amelia Knight – cosmetic designer and manufacturer based in Manchester. Among her top customers are Primark and George at Asda. The business started by creating its own brand and has now acquired rival Pascalle Cosmetics in a strategic move to significantly expand its manufacturing arm. Currently all manufacturing is based in China, and later will start in Europe as well. A key strength of the business is design and cosmetic packaging. Three brands of Amelia Knight Cosmetics are Colour Couture, Academy of Colour and Hidden Dreams.

Chatbot & Voice Assistant
We Build Bots - IntelAgent powers chatbots and voice assistants using Artificial Intelligence to help businesses save money, make money, and deliver exceptional customer service.

Concrete Layer
Concrete canvas - a flexible, concrete-filled geotexile that hardens on hydration to form a thin, durable, waterproof and fire-resistant concrete layer.

Cards
Banter Cards - Funny Cards For People With Banter. Personalised Birthday Cards, Funny Cards For All Occasions.

Car Sharing
Liftshare - Like-minded people saving money by car sharing.

Car Deals
William Loughran – deals in classic, luxury, performance and ultra-premium cars, finding rare and unobtainable cars. Provides facility for sellers to sell their cars, and arranges vehicle financing and international vehicle deliveries. At times stocks Ferrari 512 BBi, Ferrari 812 Superfast (LHD), Ferrari 488 GTB to Aston Martin B4 GT Zagato (recreation), 2007 Bugatti Veyron and Porsche Carrera 2.7 RS Lightweight (LHD).

Customer Service
Digital Engagement Centre - a Customer Engagement Centre (CEC) gathers information from different portals or channels, including various social media platforms, and provides protocols for dealing with customers by phone or in digital environments. Odigo is a smart cloud contact centre allowing customers to talk to businesses through the same channels they talk to everyone else: voice, mail, chat, text message, social and video.

Conveyancing Software
InfoTrack - conveyancing services software connects conveyancers directly to key websites used to perform conveyancing tasks, making the process fast, efficient.

Crime Investigation Software
Altia-ABM - Global specialists in crime investigation and covert operation software.

Credit Score & Reports
ClearScore - Free credit scores and credit reports.

Consumer Insight
TV Squared – more than 700 brands, agencies and networks in 70+ countries use TVSquared to measure and optimise TV, improving campaign performance by up to 80%.

D

Distribution
Henderson Foodservice - Division of the family-owned Henderson Group of companies, which has been distributing food and grocery-related products to the convenience retail sector for over 100 years.

Data & Information Consulting
Comma Group - Comma Group is an international management consultancy, and an innovative industry leader exclusively focused on data and information management.

E

Electrical Services
Declan Murock - Festive lighting, electrical services, event services and retail and wholesale of white goods, home entertainment and smart home solutions.

Energy Supplier
Spark - Spark energy is the leading energy supplier for tenants across the UK. Works with letting agents.

Ergonomic Kits
Cahoonas UK - ergonomic sportwear, baselayers, boxing gloves and fight kit.

Emotionally Nourishing Products
JustBe Botanical – a desire to restore emotional balance and enhance a sense of wellbeing. JustBe is a natural range for the face, body and home that includes spa treatments, herbal teas and chocolates. Products are emotionally nourishing and are packed full of therapeutic benefits. Every product is handmade in Scotland using purely natural ingredients. Natural aromatherapy-inspired skincare, home fragrances, organise herbal tea, and aromatherapy chocolates.

Eco-friendly Products

Kabloom – makes fun and innovative products that also happen to be eco-friendly. Designed for interaction, inspired by our relationship with nature in the urban environment. Seedboms transforms unloved spaces with a blast of life and colour! Simply throw it and grow it!

F

Farming & Food

Devenish Nutrition – Devenish is a farming and food company, delivering sustainable and innovative nutritional products and solutions for the feed industry, the food industry and for human health.

FMCG Wholesale

Pricecheck – named Export Champion, an international brand wholesaler and distributor of fastmoving consumer goods. FMCGs include cosmetics, toiletries and fragrances, food, confectionery and alcohol. Because of the sheer scale of the business, Pricecheck offers over 4500 branded products to the UK and 80 other countries. Based in Sheffield, the business plans to double its turnover to £200m.

Foreign Language

Languages 4 Life - Set up in Blackpool, the business now helps students worldwide. Offers classes for children and adults, for those learning in school and qualifications to those who just want to brush up for a holiday. It has teachers from Europe and specialises in one-on-one tuition in everything from Chinese, Polish, German, Spanish and Portuguese to English.

G

Gaming

Green Man Gaming - Game deals, games and game keys, and bundles.

Gaming

Gamely - Home of gamely games – creators of Randomise, Soundiculous and The Pretender.

H

Holidays

LoveHolidays: An example is LoveHolidays, built on the premise that customers would like to choose locations based on their own choices and preferences. Their search actually starts with the choices and preferences from LoveHolidays searches and returns tailored suggestions. LoveHolidays offers customers flexible payment options such as spreading travel costs over monthly payments.

Home and Décor

Whitemeadow – upholstery manufacturer, supplying the majority of Britain's Blue Chip High Street names and Premium Independent Retailers. It focuses on quality, style, comfort, colour and texture of the upholstery to ensure that retail customers get what suits the changing lifestyles. Whitemeadow is an independently owned business, with 100% British design and manufacturing, and full design facility. Team of designers works with expert worldwide suppliers to develop quality fabrics for use in Whitemeadow upholstery. Apart from upholstery, Whitemeadow manufactures furniture by hand at its Nottingham workshops, with new products released after obtaining UKAS certification.

Home Décor
Odddot - Designing furniture

HR
TEAMango - Outsourced HR service and change management.

Holiday Park
TY Mawr - Ty Mawr Holiday Park, Wales near Abergele and Snowdonia National Park. Great family facilities including pool and flume.

Hair-Removal Products
Cyden - Designs and manufactures Intensive Pulsed Light hair removal products for use in the home.

Healthcare
LoveBug - To improve digestive and immune health, LoveBug produces probiotics for moms and kids using cranberry extract and other ingredients.

Holiday Accommodation
Sykes Cottages – Hand-picked holiday cottages and accommodation in top locations throughout the UK and Ireland.

Hosting
Iomart - As the only UK hosting company that helps at every stage of the cloud journey. Iomart's 300+ expert consultants ensure clients stay ahead of the competition.

Heating Solutions
Adey Professional Heating Solutions - Central heating system protection and maintenance for plumbers.

I
Imaging Technology
Createc - Develop innovative applications of imaging technology.

IT
Verion 1 - IT services and solutions.

Insurance
Simply business - Tailored business insurance, including public liability, professional indemnity and landlord cover.

J

Job Site
Give a Grad A Go - Search and apply for the latest graduate jobs in London and the UK.

L

Lifestyle
UK Leisure Living – American-style hot tubs.

Logistics
Freight Logistics Solutions - Logistics solutions in the movement and alliance of freight across the UK, Europe and worldwide.

Landscaping
Maylim – specialises in hard and soft landscaping, paving projects, highways and civil engineering. Projects like Greenwich market, Tate Modern, One Tower Bridge Roof Gardens, Paddington Central Phase 2, Battersea Power Station Phase 1, The Television Centre, Canada Water Plaza, Emirates Stadium, Westfield White City, and Royal Festival Hall, all bear the name of Maylim.

Lifestyle
Guy & Beard: Shipping container barber shops. Guy & Beard is a new concept barber located in up-cycled shipping containers, providing cutting-edge barbering at affordable prices in convenient locations with free parking.

Luxury Underwear
Dick Winters – British brand of fine luxury underwear for gentlemen, exclusively made for the man who appreciates true quality and British craftsmanship. Modern British product, to actively drive the resurgence of British manufacturing, and build a sustainable and ethical British supply chain.

Luxury Lingerie
Gilda & Pearl - Luxury lingerie and loungewear.

M

Macaroons and Chocolates
Creams British Luxury is a standout brand in the luxury world of afternoon tea, cakes and patisserie. Creams has been built on experience, attention to detail, décor, surroundings, ambience, and the way it makes

customers feel. Franchisees can own the franchise and customers can enjoy the style, sophistication and luxury.

Manufacturing
CDE - designs, manufactures and commissions more wet processing plants than any other company anywhere.

Mountaineering
EverTrek - UK's No 1 Everest Base Camp specialists.

Media Content
CineMerse - We are natural-born storytellers. We understand how to craft and share your story with the world. Social Media content and video making. Worked on feature films, television shows, corporate and promotional projects across the globe.

Machining Technology
NCMT delivers high-technology engineering solutions for metal cutting and grinding applications in the UK and Europe, from stand-alone machines to complete production lines involving a high degree of automation. NCMT supplies turnkey systems covering tool setting, tooling and work holding and shop floor diagnostic products. Research and Development activities are conducted, larger turnkey systems are built and tested completely in-house prior to delivery.

Medical Research
Cytochroma - A biotechnology company that provides a flexible, reliable and ethical source of liver tissue for toxicity testing. Cytochroma accelerates new drug development by providing leading industry research organisations with the most advanced, clinically relevant stem cell-derived hepatocytes.

Musical Instruments
Lowden Guitars - Handmade and hand-built acoustic guitar range.

Nursing & Care

N

AMG Nursing: With increasing population requiring more care and constant pressure on the NHS, domiciliary care becomes the ultimate choice. AMG Nursing is a one-to-one care service for anybody wanting to stay at home, and needing minimal support through to complex nursing-led support. AMG's services are a direct alternative to residential care so that customers can stay at home. Currently focusing on Mid and North of England via nine branches, AMG covers children, adult, specialist and nursing care. Services also cover washing and dressing, taking medication, household chores and assistance with management of bills and finances.

Neurological Solutions
Nerovalens - The business works to improve the lives of those who suffer from neurological issues.

O

Organic Cotton
Cora - Personal hygiene products with certified organic cotton including organic tampons and pads. Most sales go to developing countries.

Office Fit-out
ThirdWay - The office build and design alternative – supplying commercial interior fitout and office refurbishment services in the UK.

Online Learning Materials
Alphabet Babies – develops and provide online learning material from babies to toddlers.

Organic Bibs for Children
Cheeky Chompers – cheeky dribble bibs for teething babies and more, products made from 100% organic muslin.

P

Processing Plant Manufacturers
CDE Global design, manufacture and commission wet processing plants. Wet processing of materials includes sand and aggregates, mining, C&D waste recycling, industrial sands and environmental sectors. Value proposition of the CDE is the use of highest-quality components, designing equipment to minimise running costs, creating value from waste, delivering successful wet processing projects worldwide, and continuously bringing new products to the wet processing market that improve performance and efficiency.

Project from Conception to Handover
Caukin Studio - Seeks to tackle social, environmental and economic problems through beautiful, well-crafted design through collaboration and active involvement of local communities to make an impact on everyday lives and the architectural community as a whole.

Personal Hygiene Products
Lola - Lola produces tampons, pads and condoms made with natural ingredients. Among others, investment has come from Serena Williams.

Personal Grooming
Cornerstone - Quality Razor Blades and Shaving Supplies.

Peer-to-Peer Lending Platform
RateSetter – Peer-to-peer lending platform. Its Provision Fund is an internal fund which aims to help lenders manage the risk of borrower default.

Phone, Broadband & Payments
XLN - Phone, broadband, energy and payments for small businesses.

Property Software
Zpg - Empowering smarter property and household decisions. Automated valuation model providing instant 'Zoopla estimates' for every home in the country has become a national obsession in the UK.

Paper Tissues
The Cheeky Panda – Eco-friendly range of bamboo toilet paper tissue roll and wipes, plastic-free and biodegradable.

Q

Quality Control Instruments
Stanhope-Seta - Design and manufacture quality control instruments used to measure the physical characteristics that determine product quality and consistency.

S

Sunscreen
Supergoop - Invested in by Maria Sharapova, the business makes nontoxic sunscreen by running programmes in schools.

Smart Cards
Universal Smart Cards - Design and personalise smart cards with advice on the best technology to protect and enhance use.

Skin-care & Textiles
Evolved by Nature - Started with Skin-care lines LabGrab and Silk Therpaeutics, the business now covers textiles too. Natural products are created using proteins from silkworm cocoons.

Software Manufacture
DCSL Software - Designs, develops and delivers custom software applications.

Social Housing Software
Mobysoft - Social housing intelligence software applications help landlords protect and maximise revenues, mitigate welfare reform and embed efficiencies.

Sport Content Management

Hawk-Eye Innovations - Reliable and innovative officiating solutions in sport that are changing the face of sports production, content management, and management and coaching. Services include bespoke R&D, broadcast enhancement, live production, digital, and video content management.

T

Tailoring

Suitor Brothers Tailoring – Tailor-made Suits and Formal Wear by Chris Suitor; Made-to-Measure Tailoring and Custom Bespoke Wedding Attire.

Technology

Aish technologies - Specialists in rugged display systems, electronic cabinets and cathodic protection systems for defence, marine and commercial applications.

U

Ultrasonic Products and Systems

Coltraco - Designs and manufactures range of ultrasonic products and systems focusing on liquid level indication and seal integrity testing, supported by condition-monitoring technology and after-sales servicing.

V

Virtual Reality

SenSat - lets computers understand the real world through the lens of highly detailed simulated realities, learn how things work and change the way decisions are being made. From city planning and telecommunication to autonomous vehicles, SenSat uses latest and emerging technologies by replicating real-world locations in real time, bringing clarity to complex visual and spatial data. This helps stakeholders make smarter, faster and safer decisions.

W

Wire-Stripping Machines

Laserwire – Wire-stripping machines and services; design and manufacture of laser wire strippers for precision removal and insulation from high-tech cables and wires.

Work Platforms

Niftylift - Compact and low-weight articulating booms and work platforms are a sizeable advantage in terms of safety and environmental consciousness.

Water Services

Everflow - Water supplier to UK SME businesses. Water and sewerage services.

Workflow Management

ActiveOps - Monitor, plan and optimise human and robot capacity from a single cloud solution. Compatible with all RPA, BPM, workflow, ECM and other existing systems.

Y

Yarn

Bonazzi recycles plastic-based waste material and turns it into nylon used to make upscale apparel and accessories. The company has produced Econyl thread. The yarn is now being used by Adidas AG, Levi Strauss & Co. and Speedo International.

Industry Sectors and Businesses Operating in the UK

Businesses from diversified spheres are operating in large numbers, as below:

B

Books & Publishing
Market research
School books

Beauty
Face mask manufacturer
Products manufacturer
Cosmetic designer and manufacturer
Retail

C

Clothing
Online sales
Clothing for women, men
Sports apparel

Car & Vehicles
Classic and high-performance car dealing
Wholesale and retail

Crafts
Greeting cards

Construction & Contractors
Construction and fit-out
Construction contractor
External works contractor

Conference & Events
Conference provider
Events agency

Groundwork contractor
Demolition
Housebuilder
Infrastructure supply
Construction logistics

E

Education
International schools operator
Language service provider

Engineering
Components supplier
Aircraft and spares service
Electrical and mechanical engineering

F

Food
Cheesemaker
Frozen food supplier
Catering

Fashion
Jewellery and watch retailer
Luxe goods

Financial
Financial data services
Credit hire and post-accident services

Fitness
Fitness apparel
Fitness equipment

Footwear
Sports

G

Giftware
Homeware
Glassware
Party supplies
Luxury goods

Promotional gifts

H

Hotel, Resorts
Luxury hotel operator
Luxe resort design

Horticulture
Retail
Gardening
Floristry
Landscape

I

IT, Computer, Internet, Cloud
Internet and cloud storage
IT consultancy

M

Managed services provider

Metal recycling and trading

Motor parts retailer

Music & Video
Concerts
Festivals
Online music
Video

Marketing & Promotion
Live entertainment promotion
Media agency
Digital marketing

Manufacturing
Cashmere
Textiles
Gearbox
Precision Aerospace Engineering

O

Outsourced pharmaceutical services

Online menswear retail

Orthopaedic parts maker

Online businesses
Travel agency
Cosmetics retailer
Car supermarket

P

PC supply and repair

Pet products & services

S

Suppliers
Cable supplier
Consumer goods supplier
Computer parts supplier

Software Developers
Computer games developer
Financial software developer
Fintech software developer

T

Travel
Corporate travel management
Luxury travel options
Bespoke in-country tours

W

Waste management and recycling

Y

Yachts
Luxury yacht builder
Yacht design

Disclaimer
Professional advice is essential at every step from conceiving Business Ideas to Business Launch and beyond. Readers should consider all aspects including commercial, local, national, international, market conditions, social, territorial, economic, political and personal. Suggestions made in this publication are for reference purposes only. The writer and those associated with this publication have taken reasonable care over the accuracy of the information, however, no warranty, express or implied, is given nor any liability or claim is acceptable for errors and omissions. Independent professional advice should be obtained to consider 'Which Business Should I Start in the UK?'.
....

Source
Some information in this publication has originated from reliable sources and in certain cases has been adapted. Readers are advised to access information directly from the following sources:

Office for National Statistics licensed under the Open Government Licence v.1.0.
Scottish Edge
Websites of the businesses listed

[ii] https://www.gov.uk/government/publications/why-overseas-companies-should-set-up-in-the-uk/why-overseas-companies-should-set-up-in-the-uk
[iii] https://www.gov.uk/government/publications/why-overseas-companies-should-set-up-in-the-uk/why-overseas-companies-should-set-up-in-the-uk